Restoring Order in a Chaotic World

Prayer's Foundation

Tom Dole

Ginosko House

Flowood, MS

Restoring Order In A Chaotic World
Copyright © 2019 by **Ginosko House Publishing**

All rights reserved. No part of this publication may be reproduced, distributed or transmitted in any form or by any means, without prior written permission.

Tom Dole/ Ginosko House LLC
316 Northshore Pl
Brandon MS 39047
www.ginoskohouse.com

All Scripture verses are from the New King James Version of the Holy Bible.

Book Layout © 2018 BookDesignTemplates.com

Prayer's Foundation/ Tom Dole. -- 1st ed.

Contents

A Note From The Author..1

Know the World We Live In...5

Know the Attributes of the Word of God.........................21

Know How God's Word Works..43

Know How to Pray the Word...61

APPENDICES

A. Hope: Faith Aimed At The Future..............................81

B. Attributes of God's Word: A Personal Study...............93

C. End Notes..97

ACKNOWLEDGMENTS

Special thanks are due to the following people
who gave their time, effort, and encouragement,
all of which resulted in this book:

Pastor Marcus Whitman of Whitman Ministries, and
Associate Pastor Robert Berry of Word of Life Church,
both of whom reviewed the manuscript and offered their
insights and recommendations.

My children, Bethany who formatted the manuscript for
publication, and Jeremiah who creatively designed the
Ginosko House logo.

~ DEDICATIONS~

To my wife. When the Lord said, *"He who finds a wife finds a good thing…"* He wasn't kidding. And, boy, did I! God brought a singular blessing into my life when He introduced me to Cathy, the lady who would become my wife. She brought sparkle, love, and growth into my life and into our family. The rest of that verse goes on to say, *"…and obtains favor from the Lord."*

To my children. *"Behold! Children are a heritage from the Lord…"* Jeremiah and Bethany have been to me a constant source of joy, peace, and discovery. As they experienced the life of God's creation around them, it was the light of discovery in their eyes that encouraged me to continue searching for new discoveries of my own. They taught me that the search for life's treasures should never stop. The rest of that verse goes on to say, *"…the fruit of the womb is a reward."*

To my wife and children, Cathy, Jeremiah, and Bethany. All of whom I love. Who have helped me obtain favors from the Lord in unexpected ways, and the rewards of the discoveries and adventures of life.

The blessing of the Lord, it makes one rich;
and He adds no sorrow with it.
~ Proverbs 10:22

A Note From The Author

The purpose of Ginosko House is not to "wow" people with *"persuasive words of wisdom"*,[1] but to provide foundational Scriptural knowledge and allow the Holy Spirit to "turn information into revelation." In this way, our prayer is that you will come to know the Lord more personally day-by-day.

There are many exposits and theological, philosophical definitions of the term *prayer*. Personally, I prefer "talking with God"—talking *with* God, not *to* God. Nobody likes to be talked *to*; everybody likes to talk *with* somebody. Talking with somebody implies a personal relationship to one degree or another.

That is what prayer is, or at least what it is supposed to be. For our relationship with God to be personal and two-sided (as opposed to one-sided), it must include both aspects of talking and listening. If we are doing all the talking, that is not good. We should at least be considerate enough to allow our Creator, the Lover of Our Soul, and the Sovereign of the Universe to do most of the talking.

For most of us, talking is the easy part. But that leaves us in a position of constantly wondering if God is listening. If we allow God time to speak to us, then we will have no worries as to whether or not He hears us.

Far too often, we hear people say things like, "I pray all

the time, but God never answers my prayers." Or, "Sometimes God's answer is 'No.'" Rarely, if ever, will God's answer to our prayers be a blunt "No." The real problem is this: Have we shut up long enough and learned to listen to God? Are we allowing God to talk to us and instruct us with His answer? The real question is, are we listening?

Consider Romans 10:17, *Faith comes by hearing, and hearing by the Word of God.* Hearing comes by the Word of God. We will hear God speaking to us when we study and meditate on His Word contained within the Bible. One of the jobs of the Holy Spirit is to turn information into revelation – to turn the information contained in the Bible into a revelation of how we are to live. His foremost and primary means of doing this is by speaking to us through His written Word. The Holy Spirit has a unique way of bringing the Word of God alive in our hearts. Therefore, any conversation we desire to have *with* God should combine both Bible study – listening to God, and prayer - speaking to God. When we combine Bible study and prayer, we are carrying on a conversation with God; we are both talking with and listening to the Lord. We are communicating. We are building a relationship with God.

Jesus told us, flat out, what eternal life really is:

This is eternal life, that they may know You, the only true God, and Jesus Christ, whom You have sent.[2]

Undoubtedly, the most fearful words in the Bible are these:

> *I never <u>knew</u> you.*
> *Depart from Me, you who practice lawlessness.*[3]

In these two verses, the terms *know* and *knew* are the same Greek word, *ginosko*. Ginosko means "to know by personal experience."

There will be people attempting to enter the kingdom of heaven, people who call Jesus "Lord." People who will describe to Jesus how they prophesied in His name, how they cast out demons in His name, and how they did other "signs and wonders" in His name. However, their entrance to the kingdom of heaven will be denied because Jesus doesn't *know* who they are.

All those good works they were telling Jesus about were things they did on their own. God never asked them to do those things. They never took the opportunity to spend time with God, to get to *know* Him, to find out exactly what the "good works" were "that God prepared beforehand" for them to do. They never came to *know* God; they just ran around doing their own thing.

Building a relationship takes time and practice. We have to be the ones willing to adapt and change. We can't be self-deceived. We can't run around referring to Jesus as "Lord" while, doing our own thing, even if what we're doing is considered good. We must be loyal disciples, in a genuine relationship with the Lord. Our words and actions must flow out of our relationship with Him.

So, while the title of this book indicates lessons about building a better prayer life, what it really focuses on is encouraging you to develop a better relationship with the Lord. That is why you will see the term *relationship* a lot in this book. True prayer flows out of your relationship with God.

    As you read, my prayer is that your relationship with the Lord will grow. And as your relationship with Him grows, the fruit of your prayer life increases. That *out of your heart will flow rivers of living water, the good works which God prepared beforehand that you should walk in them.*[4] So, as you enter the kingdom of heaven, you will hear these words: *"Well done, good and faithful servant."*[5]

Tom Dole

• CHAPTER 1 •

Know the World We Live In

PREACHER.

THAT IS WHAT THE WISE MAN WHO WROTE the Book of Ecclesiastes called himself. Although the Preacher taught many lessons, we will focus on just one lesson having to do with recognizing and understanding the world we live in. If we understand the world we live in, and the principles it operates by, then we can be more effective in achieving God's purposes through prayer. The Preacher begins his lessons with this observation:

> *What profit has a man from all his labor in which he toils under the sun? One generation passes away, and another generation comes.*[6]
>
> *That which has been is what will be, that which is done is what will be done, and there is nothing new under the sun.*[7]

*I have seen all the works that are done under the sun;
and indeed, all is vanity and grasping for the wind.*[8]

*Then I looked on all the works that my hands had done,
and on the labor in which I had toiled;
and indeed all was vanity and grasping for the wind.
There was no profit under the sun.*[9]

Everything we see in the world around us today has already been seen before throughout history. Technology comes and goes, but the ways in which man uses technology—for good or for evil—are always repeated throughout history. It is important for us to remember that there is nothing new under the sun.

*Of making many books there is no end,
and much study is wearisome to the flesh.
Let us hear the conclusion of the whole matter:
Fear God and keep His commandments,
for this is man's all.
For God will bring every work into judgment,
including every secret thing, whether good or evil.*[10]

Without God, the end results of all of man's efforts will only produce what the Preacher calls *vanity* – something worthless and pointless.

Know Where You Live

We live in a world that produces no lasting benefit. The profit we gain in one generation is handed down to the next generation and then passes away. All the work done under the sun rises and prospers, then fades and is replaced with something else. Kingdoms come and go, governments and corporations rise and fall, people come and go. *All is vanity and grasping for the wind.* The Preacher is not trying to paint a picture of despair. He is just pointing out the emptiness, the vanity, this world produces by itself.

When the Preacher talks about vanity, he is merely saying that the world is unstable; it is disorderly and full of confusion. It produces little of lasting value. There are reasons for that which will be discuss. The Preacher ends his lessons by pointing out that if we turn to God, we can avoid the emptiness caused by the vanity and confusion of the world.

Basic Principles of the World

The world we live in operates on what Scripture refers to as "basic principles:"

> *Beware lest anyone cheat you*
> *through philosophy and empty deceit,*
> *according to the tradition of men,*
> *according to the <u>basic principles</u> of the world,*
> *and not according to Christ.*[11]

The world has been operating on these basic principles since Adam and Eve left the Garden of Eden. As the verses referenced above indicate, the goal of these principles is to cheat all mankind. We will mentione some of these principles here. Not to generate a discussion on philosophies of life, nor to cause despair, but simply to make us aware of some principles most of the world lives by, to help us understand the vanity and confusion caused by these principles, and to understand what we should expect if we try to live by worldly principles.

We will also see, as the Preacher points out at the end of his lessons, that there is a vast difference between the vanity and confusion caused by the principles the world operates in and the order and purpose created when we live by the principles of Christ.

> *They overcame by the Blood of the Lamb,*
> *and by the Word of their testimony.*[12]

It is the application of the Word of God in our lives that gives Christians hope and victory.

The World's Basic Principles

One of the basic principles of the world is *evolutionary materialism*. This is the belief that everything we see around us—the universe itself—came about by the random chance process of evolution. Since material substance is all there is, those who live by this line of thinking become completely preoccupied with stuff. The material is all there is, so get as much as you can while the getting is good. People become fixated on material objects, things they think will provide them with comfort, status, and self-satisfaction. If they don't possess the material objects of their desire, then their primary focus and efforts are bent upon how to obtain those material objects.

Most of their industry and endeavors are spent trying to get these material things, even if the attainment is at the cost of intellectual values or even more costly, moral values. Materialistic goals can include achieving fame in the entertainment and sports industries, having a flashy car, spouting culturally acceptable ideas about society and politics, and having the clothes and styles that make us look most attractive.

While there is nothing intrinsically wrong with having such stuff, the problems arise out of the purpose for which we use these material goods. If our goal is merely the possession of "num-nums", then the material goods have controlled us and put us to work. It would be better for us to control material goods and put them to work for greater purposes. [13] But in order to do that, we need to take the time to find what the proper use of a material object is.

The issue with evolutionary materialism and the sole pursuit of things is that in the end, it always leaves us with an empty feeling, the realization that material things weren't really very important, and in gaining them we have accomplished nothing. Shouldn't there be a higher goal, a higher purpose in life? Is this all I'm here for, to grab as much stuff as I can? What's the point? It all seems so demoralizing, so confusing. As the Preacher himself points out:

> *Then I looked on all the works that my hands had done,*
> *and on the labor in which I had toiled;*
> *and indeed all was vanity and grasping for the wind.*
> *There was no profit under the sun.*[14]

Another basic principle of the world we live in is *relativism*. This principle simply states that all knowledge, morality, and truth are relative to the situations and circumstances of current cultural biases. People evaluate their situations and circumstances based on the events of their past, on different cultural and ethnic histories, or on differences in the governments they live under. Circumstances are tested based on differences in religious dogma. Relativism claims that what is true for you may not be true for me, because our circumstances are different.

Each new generation believes that it faces exciting and fearful challenges which, once overcome, will change the world. Few ever realize *that which has been is what will be, that which is done is what will be done, and there is nothing new under the sun.*[15] The reality is, every generation faces the same old challenges all previous generations have faced. When we try to resolve those challenges without God, it always results in the same vanity and confusion. Why? Because relativism makes truth highly malleable.

Living by the worldly principle of relativism involves the use of situational ethics. What is true for you may not be true for me. Okay, fine, you have your truth; I have mine.

Then, along comes a third person with a third truth for the same situation. At this point, we have divided one truth into three separate factions. How many pieces can one truth be shattered into and still be effective? A house divided against itself cannot stand. A truth divided against itself cannot stand. It is an old strategy, divide and conquer. The end result is always confusion.

One more basic principle of the world we live in is *naturalism*. Very similar to evolutionary materialism, yet with a few distinctions, this precept says that everything we see around us—including the universe itself—arose from natural causes; first there was nothing, then it exploded.

Naturalism says there were no supernatural forces or entities, no forces from outside our natural realm that were involved in the origin of all we see surrounding us. The primary goal of naturalism is to deny the existence of any supernatural force at work in the world. It allows people to deny any possible existence of God. It denies that man has a spirit that connects him to his Creator, God. Therefore, the only thing we can precisely determine is what we observe by our five *natural* senses.

This type of thinking allows men to believe they are in control of the natural forces they see around themselves; it allows for the belief that man is his own god. It is the same old lie Adam and Eve were told: *You will be like God.*[16] It is a lie containing great deception, and yet it has been believed by every generation throughout the history of mankind. And is still believed today. Scientists and bioethicists firmly believe they are going to take control of the evolutionary process and create "homo deus", the man who will never face death. Once men come to believe they are in control, then there is no need for God or God's plan or God's law. There is no need for God's order or God's unity. All of that gets shoved out of the way.

There is one primary challenge for the proponents of naturalism. If the brain of a human arose from mere natural materials, then how can we trust our thought processes? Just how adequate and reliable is a brain made from slime? Can a mind produced from natural materials produce real truth? With such an unreliable source for mental computations and deliberations, inevitably confusion will ensue. "Naturalism seems to have a built-in defeater that renders it incapable of being rationally affirmed."[17]

Vanity and Confusion

What profit has a man from all his labor in which he toils under the sun? One generation passes away, and another generation comes.[18]

These are three examples of the basic principles that guide the world we live in: evolutionary materialism, relativism, and naturalism. People pick and choose which one they want to live by as it suits their current circumstances. They switch from one to the other as it pleases them and allows for their personal self-gratification. Undoubtedly, if one of these three doesn't suit them, then there is another that can be offered for their consideration. The world is easy.

However, the bottom line is always this: it makes no difference which basic principle of the world a person chooses to operate by, they all lead to the vanity and confusion spoken of by the Preacher.

Lawlessness

The sense of hopelessness produced by vanity and confusion always leads to lawlessness. Lawlessness is basically anything involving illegality, wickedness, or violation of laws; unrighteousness. People become frustrated and angered with the hopelessness that always comes by trying to live by the world's principles. They feel cheated, just as the Scripture above said they would. And so they resort to lawlessness in an attempt to gain what they feel belongs to them.[19]

Scripture points out that Satan is the "god of this world." Therefore, he is the dominant influence in the thinking of those who strive to live by the basic principles of the world.[20] The kingdom of Satan, this world we live in, is founded upon and operates by principles of lawlessness.[21] Wherever you observe lawlessness—just check today's news articles—you are observing the kingdom of Satan in action. Lawlessness has a threefold purpose:

1. To fight against God's covenants, primarily the Abrahamic, Land, Davidic, and Blood of Christ covenants.
2. To resist the counsel of God's will as written in the Bible.
3. To promote "the lie" that we are all here by random chance; that there is no Creator and you can be your own god.

The Conclusion Of The Preacher's Lesson

*Of making many books there is no end,
and much study is wearisome to the flesh.*[22]

The Preacher summed up his lesson on vanity and confusion by pointing out that man's knowledge of the basic principles of the world may increase, and many books may be written in a never-ending attempt to expound upon the knowledge of those principles. But the value which that knowledge yields is momentary and incidental. Like situational ethics, it varies from crisis to crisis. And, the result is always "wearisome to the flesh." The result is always vanity and confusion.

*Let us hear the conclusion of the whole matter: Fear God
and keep His commandments, for this is man's all.
For God will bring every work into judgment,*

including every secret thing, whether good or evil.[23]

In distinct contrast to the vanity and confusion brought about by the world's philosophies, is the truth that *"man's all"* is found in obedience to God, in following His commandments. Pursuing a personal relationship with the God who created us is not only our purpose in this life, but it is the *only* thing that adds value to our life. All else is pointless, worthless vanity.

In The World, Not Of The World

Taking the lesson of the Preacher into consideration, Jesus made an interesting prayer to God regarding a Christian's position in the world we live in:

I do not pray that You should take them out of the world, but that You should keep them from the evil one.[24]

This is the Lord's plan. Christians are to live in a world that is ruled by the basic principles of evolutionary materialism, relativism, and naturalism, all of which lead to vanity, confusion, and lawlessness. But we are to be kept from the evil one, Satan, who is the ruler of (and, therefore, the author of) all the *"basic principles of the world."*[25] At the same time, we are to resist the effects of vanity, confusion, and lawlessness that are brought on by pursuing the basic principles of the world. Instead, we are to be *"workers together with God"*[26] in establishing His order and unity, His truth, in this world. We are to be *"ambassadors of Christ"* [27] in a world ruled by vanity, confusion, and lawlessness.

Prayer Starts Here

One of the primary ways (and in the eyes of many, *the* primary way) in which we are to function as "workers together with Him" is in prayer. First and foremost, prayer is *always* based on a relationship, a personal relationship.

There are many Scriptures that discuss prayer. Here is one most of us have heard before in regard to praying for nations:

> *If My people who are called by My name will humble themselves and pray and seek My face, and turn from their wicked ways, then I will hear from heaven, and will forgive their sin and heal their land.*[28]

We will set aside praying for the nations for a moment and look at the aspects of relationship this verse brings out. The entire context here is one of relationship. Put this verse in the background of the days of your courtship in pursuing your spouse:

Humble themselves: We did! Our desire was to do, not what we wanted to do, but whatever the love of our life desired to do, just as long as we could be in their presence.

Pray: We did, continually! Prayer is merely communication. We were on the phone—constantly!

Seek My face: Oh yes! The contortions of time-scheduling we went through were amazing, just so we could see the face of our beloved.

Turn from our wicked ways: And how! All other relationships with the opposite sex were greatly diminished, if not entirely cut off. We were pure in our pursuit of the desire of our heart.

This is what God is asking of His people, a relationship that is alive and active and vibrant. When it comes to prayer, it's all about relationship!

Ambassadorship

Let's also look at this phrase from the same passage:
If My people who are called by My name...
and compare it with this:
You shall not take the name of the LORD your God in vain, for the LORD will not hold him guiltless who takes His name in vain.[29]

Using God's name for curse words is not what is at stake here. The issue is bearing—taking on—the name of God. As a Christian, are you bearing the name of God with propriety? The issue is ambassadorship. You are supposed to be an *imager* of Christ.[30] You are supposed to "image" the moral character and nature of Jesus.

As Christians, we are not to take on the name of the Lord needlessly and uselessly. We are not to take on His name in vain, we are to be more than mere "vanity"

Christians. A vanity Christian is one who, while claiming to bear the name of Christ, still lives by the basic principles of the world. Vanity Christians bear the name of Christ in vain because, as they live by the basic principles of the world, they produce the fruit of those principles: vanity, confusion, and lawlessness.

Christians are called to be—bearing His name—true ambassadors of the Coming King. We are to be ambassadors of the King of kings who will return to Earth to overthrow Satan's kingdom of lawlessness and to establish the Kingdom of God.

As true ambassadors of Christ, we are *not to be conformed to this world, but be transfigured by the renewing of your mind, that you may prove what is that good and acceptable and perfect will of God.*[31]

Vanity Christians are easily conformed to this world and the basic precepts it operates on. True ambassadors of the Lord are *transfigured* as they renew their mind with God's Word.

Our thinking, our worldview, is to be exemplified in the precepts of the Kingdom of God: God's law, God's Word, God's righteousness. True ambassadors of Christ are to stand out in this world because they do not operate in the basic principles of vanity, confusion, and lawlessness which the world operates in.[32]

As ambassadors of Christ, we need to understand that

in the Kingdom of God righteousness has three goals. The three goals of righteousness stand in opposition to the three goals of lawlessness found in Satan's kingdom, which were previously mentioned. As ambassadors of Christ, we are to be *workers together with Him* in:

1. Establishing God's covenants (primarily the Abrahamic, Land, Davidic, and Blood of Christ covenants).
2. Fulfilling all the counsel of His will, not just cherry-picking the parts we like.
3. Promoting the Truth of His Word.

We now have some understanding of the world we live in; the world ruled by Satan's kingdom of vanity, confusion, and lawlessness. We also have some understanding of our role of living in the world, but not being of the world. We are to be fifth columnists for the Kingdom of God, as it were. And we have some understanding of the importance of being ambassadors of Christ. One of the most effective means of performing our ambassadorship is through prayer. So, let's keep *reaching forward*.[33]

Restoring Order in a Chaotic World

• CHAPTER 2 •

Know the Attributes of the Word of God

They overcame by the Blood of the Lamb, and by the Word of their testimony.[34]

IT IS THE APPLICATION OF THE WORD OF GOD in our lives that gives Christians hope and victory. That is why it is important to know the attributes of the Word of God. As Christians, we should expect God's Word to work in our lives and through our lives. Scripture states that God *upholds all things by the Word of His power.*[35] We all want God to act in our lives according to His promises, according to what He says in His Word. To live that kind of life, we must be able to believe in and act on God's Word. If we want that to happen, then it is up to us to learn the attributes of God's Word, to learn what makes God's Word work with power in our lives. Understanding the attributes of the Word of God allows us to understand the character and nature of

God. It will reveal aspects of God's character and nature for which we should give Him praise, honor, and glory. And that will help us grow in our relationship with Him.

Understanding the attributes of the Word of God will help us determine which events and situations we experience in life are from Him, and which are from other, less desirable sources. Understanding the attributes of God's Word allows us to understand the causes of events and situations in our lives. Armed with that knowledge, we can learn to apply God's Word in any situation. It teaches us how to bring a God-given resolution to those events and situations. This is one of the component pieces of prayer: bringing to bear the will of God found in His written Word as the controlling influence in a situation.

As mentioned in the previous chapter, prayer involves a relationship. Without relationship, prayer is ineffectual. As a man is known by his word, so God is known by His Word. Consider what the following Scriptures have to say about the way Words are used by God and how they should be used by men. To begin with, we need to understand that God created Heaven and Earth using His Word:

By faith we understand that the worlds were framed <u>by the Word of God</u>, so that the things which are seen were not made of things which are visible.[36]

<u>By the Word of the LORD</u> the heavens were made, and all the host of them by the breath of His mouth.[37]

Know the Attributes of the Word of God

Next, we need to understand that mankind has been created in the image of God:

> *God said, 'Let Us make man in Our image, according to Our likeness.'*[38]

> *That you put on the new man which was created according to God, in true righteousness and holiness.*[39]

> *For whom He foreknew, He also predestined to be conformed to the image of His Son.*[40]

> *We all, with unveiled face, beholding as in a mirror the glory of the Lord, are being transformed into the same image.*[41]

God creates with His Word. Because mankind is created in His image, He has also given us the ability to create using His Word. And, while we cannot create heavens and earths, we can create the circumstances of our lives by our words. Our words are like the bridle on a horse or the rudder on a ship, they steer our lives in the direction we choose.

> *Indeed, we put bits in horses' mouths that they may obey us, and we turn their whole body. Look also at ships: although they are so large and are driven by fierce wind, they are turned by a very small rudder wherever the pilot desires. Even so the tongue is a little member and boasts great things.*[42]

In any situation, the words of our mouth will build up, or

tear down:

He who guards his mouth preserves his life, but he who opens wide his lips shall have destruction.[43]

For by your words you will be justified, and by your words you will be condemned.[44]

Death and life are in the power of the tongue, and those who love it will eat its fruit.[45]

God's Word operates in the same way, just on a much more powerful scale. If the words of our mouth operate in a manner similar to the Words of God's mouth, it would be to our benefit to understand the attributes of His Word, and get our words in agreement with His Word. Then, through prayer, we can alter situations and bring them in line with the Word of God This will be the effect of our prayers if we understand the attributes of God's Word and properly apply His Word in any situation under the direction of His Holy Spirit. This is the essence of prayer.

Real Faith

Before we examine the attributes of God's Word, let's ask a question. What is faith?

You can get a lot of different answers to that question. Religious answers include, "I'm a Catholic", or "I'm a Protestant", or Muslim, or Wiccan, Hindu, etc. The problem with those answers is that they don't address the question of what faith is. They merely mention a religion of preference.

If you ask a Protestant what faith is, they will most likely refer to a denomination: Baptist, Episcopalian, Methodist, Lutheran, Unitarian, and so forth. Again, these are merely different religious sects within the Protestant religion. These answers avoid the direct question: what is faith? Faith is not a religion.

Other people will proudly affirm, "Of course I believe in God." Which, of course, has nothing to do with faith. James 2:19 admonishes them this way: *You believe that there is one God. You do well. Even the demons believe — and tremble!* No. Genuine faith involves far more than merely believing God exists.

Ask Google what faith is, and you'll get a rather strange answer to your question. Their response is that faith is a "strong belief in God, or in the doctrines *of a religion*, based on spiritual apprehension *rather than proof*."[46]

Religion does have a lot to do with "spiritual apprehension", but once again they're talking about religion, not faith. "Spiritual apprehension" results from a sense that a person does not have a proper relationship with God. All mankind is correct in that assessment. But many, attempting to repair and restore that relationship, embark on campaigns to reconcile themselves to God. Those efforts may include good works, self-sacrifice, the repetitive recitation of prayers, and so forth. The problem is, none of these efforts ever result in restoring a proper relationship with God. This is why Jesus was the most anti-religious man who ever walked the face of the earth. He understood that religion is man's own attempt to reconcile himself with God. He also understood that religion *never* restores that relationship. Religion, in fact, only serves to keep men distanced from God.

Google also adds the fact that religion—any religion—is a belief in God, but it is a belief with no proof that there really is a God. Religion – not faith – is based on something people wish to be true. On the other hand, faith, as we will soon see, provides evidence of the reality of God. Faith is God's means of drawing man to Himself for the purpose of restoring the relationship to its original status. Genuine faith is a gift from God to man. All we have to do is accept the gift. There are no "good works" or any other type of payment or penance we need to make.[47]

So, the question remains, what is faith? Faith has nothing to do with religion, and everything to do with a personal relationship. Faith is believing that a person's character and the words he speaks are true and utterly reliable. For instance, if you offer me a chair to sit in, whether or not I sit down on the chair depends on two things. First, do I trust you; do I have faith in you as being a person who is sincere and honest, or are you prone to pranks? If I trust you as a person, I am more likely to sit down.

Second, do I trust your words, do I have faith in what

Know the Attributes of the Word of God

you say? Do I have faith in your words? You may have verbally offered me a seat, but if by looking at the condition of the chair I see it appears to be unstable, then I am less likely to trust—to have faith in—your Words. I will most likely look for another chair to sit in.

My actions will bear out two things: 1) my faith in your character, and 2) my faith in your Words. My actions are evidence of my faith in you, who you are and what you say. Notice that faith always results in action of one type or another. Either I "believe in you" and sit down, or I do not "believe in you" and remain standing.

If I am in the process of building a relationship with you, then my faith in you—how you behave in different situations, whether what you say is trustworthy and reliable—will grow over time. Or not, if your words prove untrustworthy. If I have faith in you, then I will trust what you say to me, and I will act on what you tell me. My actions will bear out my faith in the reliability of your character and your Words. The more experience we have together, the more my faith in you will grow... or not.

Just as in the example of sitting in the chair, learning to have faith in God requires a personal relationship. In the same manner, when we say we have faith in God, we are not merely saying that we believe in God, or that we believe God exists, or that we are a member of some type of religious group. What we are really saying—or really should be saying—is that based on a personal relationship with the Creator of the Universe, we have found His character and nature, as well as His Word, to be utterly reliable and trustworthy. We can trust—have faith—in who He is and in what He says. Our faith in God and in His Word is acted on in our lives and produces the results God said it would produce.

In fact, we can have so much faith in who He is and in what He says that we order our entire life around God and His Word. When God offers us a chair to sit in, we can completely trust His character to be such that He will not prank us and pull the chair out from under us. Furthermore, we can completely trust His Word that the chair is structurally safe to recline in. Therefore, we can act on who God is and what He says, and we can safely and comfortably sit in the chair.

So, what is faith? Faith is believing in the character of God and the veracity of His Word to where you order your life according to His Truth. It only makes sense, and should be plainly clear, that faith requires a personal and living relationship with God.

Building a proper relationship takes time. Building a relationship with God requires spending time with Him on a regular and consistent basis so that you know and understand that God will fulfill and perform His Word, just as He says He will in Scripture. As your relationship with

God grows, you come to know by experience that His character and nature are completely trustworthy.

Our First Experience with Faith

The purposes of God, along with His character and His nature, are made known in His Word. Our challenge is understanding God's Word without getting all theological and philosophical about it. Theology is the study of God; it is an attempt to learn *about* God. True faith requires *knowing* God personally. That's a big difference! Too many theologians know about God, but do not really know God personally. Philosophy won't help much either, it is merely the study of knowledge. Too many people know about knowledge, yet do not have any.

Real faith is exemplified in a person when they are born again. Most Christians understand that there were no works, good deeds, or anything else they could have done in order to impress God so much so that He would be compelled to redeem them and bring them to heaven.

For all have sinned and fall short of the glory of God.[48]

What fruit did you have then in the things of which you are now ashamed? For the end of those things is death. For the wages of sin is death, but the free gift of God is eternal life in Christ Jesus.[49]

At some point, we all realized that there was not a thing we could do to earn salvation. Remember: any kind of attempt to earn our salvation is nothing more than religion.

Jesus hates religion because it never leads anyone to *know* God. As we struggled to find a solution to our predicament, knowing that the solution was not in ourselves, we attempted to find an answer in the Bible. We either read the Bible ourselves or went to a place where we could hear it taught. Once we heard that God had provided Jesus as the sacrificial Lamb of God to pay the penalty for all of our wrongdoings, we began a search to find out how to appropriate this benefit for our own situation. At some point, we read or heard what God said in Romans 10:9-10, that if we *believe in our heart that God raised Jesus from the dead*, and say with our mouth, 'Jesus be my Lord', *we will be saved.*

We took those Words in faith, believing that they represented the character and nature of God, believing that He loved us so much He was willing to have His own Son suffer the punishment which we should have suffered. We took those Words in faith, believing that what God said in those Words was true and dependable. And we acted on those Words. We believed in our heart that God raised Jesus from the dead, and we spoke with our mouth asking Jesus to be our Lord. And we were born again. Our relationship with the Lord was restored. That is faith in action.

The bottom line is this: We trusted the character and nature of God to be honest and upright. We believed what God said in His Word to be true and reliable. We acted on what He said and discovered that God is true to Himself and to His Word. We received what God said we would receive – His salvation. That is true faith.

Part of the problem some people have is that they stop here, they quit building the relationship. They have been born again, but they quit pursuing a closer relationship with the God of Life. Notice that to be born again, we had to do some searching to find out what God's Word had to say about resolving the issues we faced. After that initial search, some are unwilling to be diligent in continuing the process of building their relationship with God. They quit searching for other promises in His Word. They become "vanity Christians", Christians in name only, not having a vital active relationship with their Lord.

But for those who are willing to continue their pursuit of God, being born again is only the first step. The next steps of growing in faith involve learning and understanding the attributes of God's Word. What is it about the Word of God that will allow us to put our trust in it? If we understand the attributes of the Word of God, we will understand the character and nature of God Himself.

Becoming a Faith Builder

Now that we have an understanding of what true faith is, and an understanding that true faith requires having a viable, dynamic relationship with God, we come to the next question: How do we build our faith?

That was the request Jesus' disciples made, *Lord, increase our faith.*[50] Jesus' response to His disciples was to instruct them in how to use God's Word in actions of faith:

If you have faith as a mustard seed, <u>you can say</u> to this mulberry tree, 'Be pulled up by the roots and be planted in the sea,' and it would obey you.[51]

Notice how His lesson on faith emphasizes how we use our Words. Jesus' teaching is reinforced by Paul:

Faith comes by hearing, and hearing by the Word of God.[52]

Simply stated, a person's faith grows by hearing the Word of God, believing it – believing God says what He means and means what He says - and then by talking and living by the Word of God. Faith grows by spending time with God in His Word each day. Just like any relationship you build with anyone else, it requires time spent together, time spent getting to know each other. We build a relationship with someone by spending time with them, listening to what they say, and observing how they behave in various situations to see if they do what they say. It is the same with God. And remember, He will also be observing you, to see if He can trust you to live by His Word. Relationships are always a two-way street. They require genuine interest and genuine effort.

Building the Relationship

Once we are born again, we have to continue building our relationship with God. God has chosen to reveal Himself to us through His written Word. Therefore, if we are going to increase our faith in God and His Word, it is important that we allow the Holy Spirit to lead us in a study of the attributes of the Word of God.

Eternal life is *knowing* God.[53] The more we know about the Word of God, the more we know about His character and nature. Understanding the character and nature of God will help us grow in our faith and in learning to trust in what He says. As we begin to grow in our relationship with God, we will begin to order our life more and more by His Word. We will put action to our faith that what He says in His Word is true.

As we study God's Word, we will find more of His promises contained within it. Just as we experienced the reliability of His Word regarding salvation, we can believe He will also be faithful in His other promises. Our increasing faith will allow us to appropriate those promises into our lives through prayer and obedience.

Through the process of building a proper relationship with God, our character and nature begin to become more like His. As we act on His Word in faith, and order more and more of our life according to His Word, we become an "imager" of Jesus Christ.

For whom He foreknew, He also predestined to be conformed to the image of His Son, that He might be the firstborn among many brethren.[54]

But we all, with unveiled face, beholding as in a mirror the glory of the Lord, are being transformed into the same image from glory to glory, just as by the Spirit of the Lord.[55]

Since you have put off the old man with his deeds, and have put on the new man who is renewed in knowledge according to the image of Him who created him.[56]

My little children, for whom I labor in birth again until Christ is formed in you.[57]

Attributes of the Word of God

The Apostle Paul teaches us that we can increase our faith by hearing—studying and meditating—the Word of God. One of the best ways to do this is to begin a personal study of the attributes and characteristics of God's Word. What is it in God's Word that makes it so reliable? What is it that makes God's Word work? What are the attributes of the Word of God that will help us increase our faith? The guy who wrote Proverbs put it this way:

That I may make you know the certainty of the Words of truth.[58]

What are the attributes of the Word of God that will make us know the certainty of the Words of truth? There's a two-fold aspect in this type of study. First, and of primary importance is this: you get to know a person by talking with them and by learning the substance of what they say. Remember that in our relationship with God, being born again is merely the first step. As children of the Living God, our primary aim is getting to know God and His Son Jesus Christ much more intimately.

Second, this type of study helps us to *"know the certainty of the Words of truth."* It helps us to understnd that God says what He means and means what He says. And that He will do what He says. That understanding helps us to grow in applying God's Word to the circumstances of our lives.

The Example of Pruning

The more we know the certainty of the Words of truth, the more change it will bring in our lives. God's calls this process of change *pruning*. Jesus taught us about the process of pruning in John 15:1-8:

I am the True Vine, and My Father is the vinedresser. Every branch in Me that does not bear fruit He takes away; and every branch that bears fruit He <u>prunes</u>, that it may bear more fruit.
You are already <u>clean</u> because of the Word which I have spoken to you. Abide in Me, and I in you.

As the branch cannot bear fruit of itself unless it abides in the vine, neither can you, unless you abide in Me. I am the vine, you are the branches. He who abides in Me, and I in him, bears much fruit; for without Me you can do nothing.

If anyone does not abide in Me, he is cast out as a branch and is withered; and they gather them, and throw them into the fire, and they are burned. If you abide in Me, and My Words abide in you, you will ask what you desire, and it shall be done for you. By this My Father is glorified, that you bear much fruit; so you will be My disciples.

Notice carefully that the Greek term for the Word "prunes" in verse two is *kathario*. It simply means "to cleanse."

In the very next verse, Jesus tells us we are *already clean because of the Word which I have spoken to you.* The Greek term for the Word "clean" in this verse is also *kathario*, exactly the same as the word for "prune" in the previous verse. Jesus is telling us that the Father's pruning process involves us making adjustments in our lives according to what we learn as we study His Word. The lesson Jesus is teaching us is this: the Word of God will tell us what elements to bring into our lives, and what elements to remove from our lives. That is God's pruning process. We will take a little deeper look into this in the next chapter.

So, as you progress in this study, remember that we're not just wanting to know *about* God's Word—we want to know God *by* His Word. We need to know, and know by personal experience, the reliability of what God says in His Book. This is how we increase our faith. It is important for a Christian to have faith in the authenticity of the Word of God. We need to know, by personal experience, by a personal relationship with God, the *certainty of the Word of truth*. In order to do that, we must understand the attributes of God's Word.

There is one more element that will help us in our understanding of how God's Word is applied in prayer and the various situations we face in life.

The *Logos* and the *Rhema*

One of the things you will discover, in both the Old Testament Hebrew and New Testament Greek, is that there are two different concepts for the term "Word". In the Old Testament, the two terms for Word are *dabar* and *imrah*. In the New Testament, the two terms are *logos* and *rhema*.

Dabar and *logos* essentially mean the same thing. They both refer to the entire discourse on every aspect of a matter. The term *dabar* in the Old Testament and *logos* in the New Testament both refer to the complete expressions of God's thoughts and speech. They are the complete expression of who God is and how He deals with mankind. They are the complete communication from God to Man concerning everything that God has to do with Man. Another way of saying this is that *dabar* and *logos* refer to the whole counsel of God.

On the other hand, the terms *imrah* and *rhema* refer to a portion of the *dabar/logos* which applies to a specific situation. *Imrah* corresponds to *dabar* in the Old Testament.

Rhema corresponds to *Logos* in the New Testament. The authority and reliability of the *imrah/rhema* comes from the *dabar/logos*. A Word of *imrah/rhema* calls forth faith. It tells us how God views the situation and what He will do to set the situation in order. A Word of *imrah/rhema* tells us specifically how to apply God's *dabar/logos in* a given situation. It tells us how to live, and act in order to have God's victory in the situation.

Verbally confessing our faith in God and His Word, in speech and in action, brings forth life—His life! If we know *the certainty of the Word of truth*, then we can stand in prayer on the *imrah/rhema* given to us by His Holy Spirit. The most important thing to remember is this: we cannot choose which part of God's Word we want to work for us. He will tell us what part of His Word to apply in each situation. Therefore, having a living, vital relationship with God is required!

Occasionally, in the Old Testament, you will find *dabar* and *imrah* juxtaposed, just as you will find *logos* and *rhema* are in the New Testament. As you study God's Word and learn to live by its precepts, it will be important for you to know which term for Word is being used, *dabar* or *imrah*, *logos* or *rhema*. Is the verse talking about the entirety of God's message to Man, or is the verse talking about a piece of that message which can be properly applied to a specific situation?

Know the Attributes of the Word of God

Getting Started

Let's begin our study of the attributes and characteristics of the Word of God. We will consider just a few scripture verses here that instruct us about various attributes of God's Word. The rest is up to you. No one else can develop your relationship with God. You have to spend time with Him.

God's Word is Alive

Hebrews 4:12 emphasizes this particular aspect of the Word of God:

For the Word of God is living and powerful, and sharper than any two-edged sword, piercing even to the division of soul and spirit, and of joints and marrow, and is a discerner of the thoughts and intents of the heart.

The Word of God is *living*. It's alive and active. This is confirmed in John chapter one, verses one and three, where it says Jesus is the Word and in Him is the life. It is also confirmed in the first chapter of Genesis, where it is the Word spoken by God which creates all the life we see around us. Additionally, Acts 12:24 says, *The Word of God grows and multiplies.* Growth and multiplication are both functions of life.

Hebrews 4:12 tells us, *The Word of God is...powerful.* This is confirmed in Acts 19:20: *So the Word of the Lord grew mightily and prevailed.* All these Scriptures associate the functions of life—living, growing, multiplying, strength, and vigor—with the Word of God. And why not; Jesus is the Living Word (John 1:1-3). Jesus Himself instructs us about the life-giving seed that is the Word of God:

> *Now the parable is this: The seed is the Word of God...*[59]

There are seven other verses in Scripture that directly relate life with the Word of God, but the search to discover those verses will be left up to you.

God's Word Is Firmly Established

Psalm 119:89 tells us,

> *Forever, O Lord, Your Word is settled in heaven.*

At least in heaven, God's Word is irrefutable and beyond doubt. In heaven, there is no other Word that stands in opposition to, or as an alternative to, the Word of God. Isaiah 40:8 reiterates the same understanding:

> *The grass withers, the flower fades,*
> *but the Word of our God stands forever.*

We need to understand the emphasis God places on this attribute of His Word. God's Word lasts until new government leaders are elected, or until cultural norms change. No! God's Word lasts *forever*! If it was true for one generation, it's true for the next generation. Circumstances may change, leaders come and go, but God's Word does not change. Governments, kingdoms, and civilizations rise and fall, but God's Word is the same for each one of them. There is absolute truth, and that truth is found in the Word of God. God's Word is truth, and the truth contained in it does not change.

God's Word Never Fails to Accomplish Its Purpose

Tied in with the understanding that God's Word never changes, no matter the circumstances, we find this lesson in Isaiah 55:11:

So shall My Word be that goes forth from My mouth; it shall not return to Me void, but it shall accomplish what I please, and it shall prosper in the thing for which I sent it.

God's Word never fails. God's Word never returns to Him empty or only partially fulfilled. God's Word always accomplishes the purpose for which He spoke it. And it doesn't just accomplish His purpose half-heartedly, or in a "that's good enough" manner. It always completes the full scope of all that God intended.

The only question we should have is this: will we get in agreement with what God says, in our words and actions and will we be there to see His Word come to pass? If we are going to be victorious in prayer, we must have a firm understanding of this principle. Some prayers are made over the long haul. We must be persistent in our faith and understanding that God says what He means, means what

He says. We must be entirely confident that in due time God's Word will accomplish His purpose.

Continuing ...

These are just a very few of the Scriptures that instruct us about the attributes of God's Word. What is really required on your part is to do your own study on the attributes of the Word of God. *You* have to grow in your relationship with the Lord. No one can do it for you.

As Christians, we are exhorted to *continue in the faith*.[60] Now that we know what faith is, we know what we need to do to continue in it. We also know that the true value of "continuing in the faith" lies in building a strong relationship with the Lord, by communicating with Him through His written Word.

In Appendix A, you will find one hundred verses containing information on different attributes of the Word of God. But there are so many others. Look each one up, write them down, meditate on them, learn who God is, and begin living by His Word. Get to know God personally! And as you do, our prayer is that His *rivers of living water* will begin to flow in you and through you!

• CHAPTER 3 •

Know How God's Word Works

NOW THAT WE'VE BEGUN THE PROCESS of understanding the attributes of the Word of God, and the process of growing in our relationship with the Lord, it is time to learn how God's Word works. One of the ways we can begin to learn this is by observing the following lessons in the Bible.

The Value and Priority God places on His Word

Just off the top of our heads, most of us would probably say God places a lot of value and a high priority, on His Word. We would be correct in our assessment. But just how great is a lot, and how lofty is high?

We spend much time in praise and worship, declaring the glory and the honor of God, His power, His holiness, His mercy and grace, His wisdom, and especially His name.

And we should. Many of the Psalms encourage us in this. For example:

> *I will extol You, my God, O King;*
> *and I will bless Your name forever and ever.*
> *Every day I will bless You, and I will praise Your name*
> *forever and ever. Great is the LORD, and greatly to be*
> *praised; and His greatness is unsearchable.*[61]

In the Book of Acts, we see people healed through faith in the name of Jesus.[62] We are also told *that at the name of Jesus every knee should bow, of those in heaven, and of those on earth, and of those under the earth.*[63] And bow they will, because the name of Jesus is the name above all names.[64]

The Foundation of Power in the Lord's Name

However, in order to refine our praise and worship of the Lord, we should give more serious consideration to this lesson in Psalm 138:1-2:

> *I will praise you with my whole heart;*
> *before the gods I will sing praises to You.*

Proper praise and worship requires the use of our whole heart, even in the presence of other gods. We are to praise our God above all others.

> *I will worship toward Your holy temple,*
> *and praise Your name...*

This is a good practice to develop. We should all worship the Lord and give Him the honor and the glory due to His name.

... for Your lovingkindness and Your truth ...

Isn't God's love wonderful? And aren't we glad that God tells us the truth? Yes, and yes! But the last line in verse two tells us why our praise and worship require our whole heart. It tells us why we should exalt the Lord above all other gods and why we should praise His name in glory and honor. It tells us why His lovingkindness and truth are so wonderful:

For You have magnified Your word above all Your name.

Whoa! Wait! What? God places greater value and a higher priority on His Word as compared to His name? Why would God place greater value and a higher priority on his Word rather than on His name?

Taqiyya & Machiavelli

In the Muslim religion, it is okay to lie if it will help advance the cause of Islam. That would be one reason the god of Islam is not the same as the God of the Bible. The Islamic principle of lying is called *taqiyya*. It is okay to lie in order to hide your faith among non-believers. It is okay to lie in order to appear friendly to non-Muslims, even though you are really unfriendly. There are several other examples in the Quran about when it is okay to lie.

Interestingly, in Western culture, there is a principle of falsehood that is very similar to that of Islamic *taqiyya*. It is based on the principles of Machiavellianism. Simply put, it allows a leader in government, business, religion, or other endeavors, to never keep his word "when by doing so it would be against his interests."[65] Or, as Niccolò Machiavelli stated more succinctly, "A leader never lacks legitimate reasons to break his promise."[66] Machiavelli also said, "The promise given was a necessity of the past: the word broken is a necessity of the present."[67] In either case, whether taqiyya or Machiavellianism, the bottom line is that the end justifies the means. It is okay to use immoral, illegal methods, as long as it produces something considered to be beneficial to the one doing the lying.

Most leaders we have today, whether in governments, businesses, the judicial system, the news media, education, or society—and even in religion—are all similar to the rulers found in biblical times. It is very common for leaders to use their own authority to break laws and rules and to violate their own promises. Just as the despotic rulers of ancient times did, many of today's leaders consider themselves to be above the law.

Today we live in a world where Muslim culture is ruled by taqiyya, and Western culture, unfortunately including much of Christianity, is ruled by Machiavellianism. But, for our God, Yahweh, the God of the Bible, it is *never* okay to lie.

Know How God's Word Works

> *Lying lips are an abomination to the LORD,*
> *but those who deal truthfully are His delight.*[68]
>
> *He who works deceit shall not dwell within My house;*
> *he who tells lies shall not continue in My presence.*[69]

Most of us understand that the name of God represents His authority. We pray in the name of the Lord and people are baptized in the name of the Father, the Son, and the Holy Spirit. The episode in Acts, mentioned above, tells us people are healed in the name of Jesus. The name of God represents His authority, His influence, and His character.

However, when God declares that He magnifies His Word above all His name, He is differentiating Himself from other gods and from corrupt leaders who use their authority to break laws, rules, and promises. These gods and leaders are usually breaking the laws, rules, and promises which they made, and which they expect everyone else to obey. But God is declaring that He exalts His Word above His own authority, and that He lives by His own rules and laws. He declares He will never, under any circumstances, break, violate, or rescind His Word. God keeps His promises.

This is a critical principle to understand if we are to place our faith and trust in God and His Word,. If God's Word has no value, then neither does His name. If there is no power in His Word, then there is no authority in His Name. Why is there authority in the name of the Lord?

Because He keeps His Word. He *watches over His Word to perform it.*[70]

God is not a man, that He should lie, nor a son of man, that He should repent. Has He said, and will He not do? Or has He spoken, and will He not make it good?[71]

There is no God like our God. Our God is completely trustworthy, and so is His Word. As for men's word… well, remember what James 3:2-12 said.

For we all stumble in many things.
If anyone does not stumble in word, he is a perfect man, able also to bridle the whole body.

Indeed, we put bits in horses' mouths
that they may obey us, and we turn their whole body.
Look also at ships:
although they are so large and are driven by fierce winds, they are turned by a very small rudder
wherever the pilot desires.

Even so the tongue is a little member
and boasts great things.
See how great a forest a little fire kindles!
And the tongue is a fire, a world of iniquity.

The tongue is so set among our members
that it defiles the whole body,
and sets on fire the course of nature;
and it is set on fire by hell.

Know How God's Word Works

*For every kind of beast and bird, of reptile
and creature of the sea, is tamed
and has been tamed by mankind.*

*But no man can tame the tongue.
It is an unruly evil, full of deadly poison.*

*With it we bless our God and Father,
and with it we curse men,
who have been made in the similitude of God.
Out of the same mouth proceed blessing and cursing.
My brethren, these things ought not to be so.*

*Does a spring send forth fresh water and bitter
from the same opening?
Can a fig tree, my brethren, bear olives,
or a grapevine bear figs?
Thus no spring yields both salt water and fresh.*

That's the difference between God and His Word and men and their word. Psalm 138:1-2 has provided us with a critical piece of information about the value God places on His Word: *You have magnified Your Word above all Your Name.* James 3:2-12 has given us some insight into the value of man's word. We will rely on this lesson, not just in our prayer life, but also in our personal relationship with the Lord.

Imagers

For true Christians, the situations we face when the issue is the Word of God vs. man's word involves our personal character. Specifically, it involves the character of

God and how we, as Christians, are should properly represent His character in the world.

As born-again Christians, we are supposed to be imagers of Jesus and of His moral character. Lying, breaking promises, using your personal authority to break your own word, along with any other type of immoral behavior, is an element of man's sin nature. It is not a characteristic of God's nature. It doesn't make any difference what the motivation for immoral actions might be, nor what the outcome, good or bad, might be. People, Christians included, have a tendency to practice situational ethics. If by breaking God's Word, or their own word, through lying or some other duplicitous conduct, they think they can bring about some intended benefit or good, they will do so. Their reasoning is that the ends justify the means.

Breaking God's commands found in His Word, is never a reflection of the character and nature of God, whom we as Christians are called upon to image. God's laws prohibit lying. Period. God never said, 'You shall not lie… unless there is some overriding benefit or good to be gained." In God's law, there are no allowances for situational ethics; no end ever justifies the means for breaking His Word or our word.

As He who called you is holy,
you also be holy in all your conduct, because it is written,
'Be holy, for I am holy.' [72]

The value God places on His Word is the same value born-again Christians should place on His Word, and on their own word. This lesson underlines the importance of knowing the attributes of the Word of God. This lesson also makes clear to us the power of the Word God as it is applied in prayer.

How God Uses His Word

In the first chapter of Genesis, you can read the account of God's work at Creation. The account describes the events that took place on each of the seven days of Creation, and what was created on each of those days. It is important to notice that the tool God used to perform the work of Creation was His Word. He spoke Creation into existence. This is confirmed in Hebrew 11:3,

*By faith we understand
that the worlds were framed by the word of God,
so that the things which are seen
were not made of things which are visible.*

and in Psalm 33:6:

*By the word of the LORD the heavens were made,
and all the host of them by the breath of His mouth.*

This statement by itself shows the power contained within God's Word. From the previous chapter, you will also remember Acts 12:24,

The word of God grew and multiplied.

and Acts 19:20,

So the word of the Lord grew mightily and prevailed.
Both verses tell us that the Word of God is filled with life-giving power. To these verses we will add Hebrews 1:3:

... upholding all things by the word of His power.

These verses increase our understanding of the power and authority of the Lord Jesus Christ, who truly *"upholds all things by the Word of His power..."* Not only did God create the universe with His Word, He still holds it all together with His Word, even today.

The first four verses of Hebrews and the first four verses of the Gospel of John make a remarkable study on the character, nature, and purpose of Jesus. Jesus lives by, speaks by, and does everything by the Father's Word. This is why John 1:14 says, *The Word became flesh and dwelt among us.* (By the way, the term "word" in Hebrews 1:3, is that *logos* or *rhema*? What about Acts 12:24 and 19:20? What could you learn about prayer and about God by the differences in usage? Just a little treasure hunt for the diligent.)

What we really need to focus on is the understanding that the power contained in God's Word is what upholds all of Creation. All of Creation is held together and moves in all of its orderly processes - which can be studied and observed - because of the power contained within the Word of God. Now, that's power!

Let's get back to Genesis so we can learn how God's Word works, and how we can properly apply its power in our lives and in our prayers.

Genesis 1:3, refers to the events that occurred in Day One of the six days in which God created the Heavens and the Earth. In this verse, we find the phrase *the evening and the morning were the first day*. The same phrase—*the evening and the morning*—is repeated for days two through six. So, in each of the first six days of Creation, God went through the process of *the evening and the morning*. Please note that each of the first six days of Creation began with evening and ended with morning, not with the usual progression of morning to evening we are familiar with. We should also take note that the same phrase, the evening and the morning, is not used in reference to Day Seven. This should cause us to wonder what lesson the Holy Spirit has for us in these verses.

In this phrase, *"the evening and the morning,"* the Hebrew term for evening is *erev*, and the Hebrew term for morning is *boqer*. We should note that "evening" was not the original meaning of the term *erev*, nor was "morning" the original meaning for the term *boqer*. From Strong's Concordance, here are the original meanings of these two terms:

Erev

Erev means obscuration and mixture. It refers to encroaching darkness, which denies us the ability to discern shape, form, and identity. The image of increasing darkness and obscurity at twilight is probably why the word later came to mean evening. It is the obscuration caused by *erev* that causes things to be less discernible. *Erev* causes things to be disorderly and chaotic, it causes things to become confusing.

Boqer

Boqer means to become discernible, the perception of order. *Boqer* refers to relief from the obscurity and confusion caused by *erev*. *Boqer* is the ability to discern shapes, forms, and identities due to the breaking forth of light. *Boqer* provides the information required to see things clearly so they can be put in order. The image of increasing light and perception at dawn is probably why the word later came to mean morning.

In a scientific sense, we can view *erev* as increasing entropy and *boqer* as decreasing entropy. I'm sure everyone remembers, from your high school science classes, what the term entropy refers to. But just in case too many years have passed by since high school...

Entropy refers to the increasing disorder and chaos that is caused by a decrease in information. Catch that: *a decrease in information causes an increase in disorder and chaos*. Whatever causes something to become disorganized, to decay and degenerate, to break up and collapse, would be caused by the forces of entropy—*erev*—removing information.

The opposite of entropy would be an increase in information resulting in increased order, organization, and unity. An increase in information causes a decrease in entropy, a decrease in disorder and chaos.

If *boqer* - order, unity, information, and truth - is increased, then *erev* - disorder, chaos, misinformation, and lies - is decreased. Conversely, if *boqer* is decreased, then *erev* is increased. With this understanding of the meaning of the terms *boqer* and *erev*, we can see how God used His Word during the process of Creation.

During each of the first six days of Creation, God removed a little bit of *erev* - disorder, chaos, misinformation, and lies -and added a little more *boqer* – God's order, unity, information, and truth. Each day of Creation contained less *erev* and more *boqer*. Finally, by the end of Day Six, the process was complete. There was no *erev* left to remove, and no need to add more *boqer*. All of Creation was a complete, unified, self-sustaining system. Therefore, in Day Seven, the phrase *the evening and the morning* - the *erev* and the *boqer*- is not used. God's Creation was complete and self-sustaining. It was perfect. God was finished with the work of Creation.

God's Word Works!

God accomplished this entire act of Creation by His Word over a six-day period. God used His Word to remove a little *erev* and add a little *boqer* each day until His will and purpose was finished and complete. There is power in the Word of God! This is why God magnifies His Word above all His name. The power in the Word of God is what puts authority in His Name.

What we desire in our prayer life is the power of God's Word to accomplish His will and His purposes. Prayer is the application of God's Word into a situation so that it removes the *erev* - the disorder, chaos, misinformation, and lies - and restores God's *boqer* - His order, unity, information, and truth. If, as imagers of Christ, we learn to value and honor the Word of God, we will see the Word of God work in our lives and through our lives.

The Return of *Erev*

Creation remained in a self-sustaining state of *boqer* - order and unity - until Adam and Eve rebelled. Adam and Eve had been given authority over God's Creation. But when they made the decision to rebel against the Word of God, so much damage was done to the order and unity of God's Creation that it fell back into a state of entropy and decay. Adam and Eve displaced the Holy Spirit-empowered *boqer* found in the truth of God's Word and replaced it with the *erev* found in the word of Satan's lie. All of Creation fell into a constant state of *erev*—disorder, chaos, misinformation, and lies —under the ruler of this world, Satan.

If you stop to think about how the fall took place, you'll realize that Satan introduced his *erev* by way of a lie, by introducing a word of *erev* that stood in opposition to the *boqer* of God's Word. He told Eve a lie; he gave her a word of *erev*, a word of misinformation. Unfortunately, when it came to choosing between the *boqer* of the Word of God and the *erev* of the word of Satan, Adam and Eve made the wrong choice was made. Adam and Eve believed the lie of the word of Satan over the truth of the Word of God. Disorder, chaos, misinformation, and lies ensued. In effect, Adam and Eve canceled out the authority of the life-sustaining *boqer* in the Word of God which only produces order, unity, information, and truth, and brought in the *erev* of the word of Satan, which only produces disorder, chaos, misinformation, and lies.

The World We Live In

In the world we live in since the Fall, everything tends toward entropy, a state of *erev*. We must constantly make efforts to maintain *boqer*. Think about it. If you straighten out the hall closet today, you're adding *boqer* in an effort to remove *erev*. But in one week's time, you will open the door to the hall closet only to find that *erev* has increased. Things are not quite at the same degree of order and unity which you restored last week. And until you repeat the process of adding *boqer* to the hall closet again, the *erev*, the disorder and chaos, will only grow worse.

We live in a world that operates under the Law of Entropy, or the Second Law of Thermodynamics for you science buffs. Everything in our world, and in the universe, naturally tends towards a state of entropy: a state of disorder, of chaos, of lies and misinformation. It takes effort—work and diligence—on our part to reverse the process of entropy and maintain a state of order, unity, information, and truth.

Every lie a person tells promotes the enemy's goal of increasing disorder and chaos. This is the primary reason God prohibits lying, no matter what the circumstances are. We must constantly be aware that God has magnified His Word above all His name and, therefore, He will never use His authority to override His Word or His promises. We must understand we are called to be imagers of Christ and that we must place the same value on God's Word that He does. Remember what Jesus said, *For every idle word men may speak, they will give account of it in the day of judgment.*[73] Ouch!

Isn't this why Jesus also told us, *Man shall not live by bread alone, but by every word that proceeds from the mouth of God.*[74] In order for us to overcome the *erev* we find everywhere in the world around us, we need the *boqer* of the Word of God to restore His order, His unity, His Truth, and His information in our lives. This is what should distinguish the life of the Christian from the life of those living by the principles - the *erev* - of the world.

What was Jesus talking about when He told us to let our light shine and not hide it under a bushel basket?[75] He was talking about the light that shines from the *boqer* of God's Word as it works in us and through us.

> *The entrance of Your words gives light;*
> *it gives understanding to the simple.*[76]

God's Word removes the darkness and restores the light. The entrance of the Word of God into our lives brings with it the light we need to discern the *erev*, and to restore God's *boqer*. As we learn to live by God's Word, the light of the *boqer* of God's Word begins to shine through our life into the darkness of the world around us.

Just as it did during the six days of Creation, the entrance of God's Word into our lives, which implies that we actually have a relationship with the Lord and are sitting daily at His feet receiving His Word and applying it to our lives, removes the *erev*, the disorder and the chaos, and increases the *boqer*, God's order and unity, in our lives - spirit, soul, and body.

Restoring Order in a Chaotic World

• CHAPTER 4 •

Know How to Pray the Word

REAL PRAYER IS BUILT UPON a proper relationship with God. Prayer will not work well, if at all, without a living and vital relationship with God. Out of that relationship will grow our understanding of the elements we discussed in the first three chapters: the world we live in, the attributes of the Word of God, the power God can put in His Word (if we misuse God's Word He will put no power in it), and how God's Word works. In this chapter, we will focus on properly applying the Word of God in prayer.

All real prayer involves the removal of the *erev*—the disorder, chaos, misinformation, and lies of Satan's word, and the restoration and increase of the *boqer* —the order, unity, information, and truth of God's Word in any situation. Prayer involves a process similar to what God performed at Creation. In prayer God is allowing us to be involved in His process, He is allowing us to be *workers together with Him*.[77]

Workers Together

Let's consider this aspect of prayer. It is our relationship with God in prayer that allows us to become workers together with Him. Most of us are familiar with the following verse:

> *For by grace you have been saved through faith,*
> *and that not of yourselves; it is the gift of God,*
> *not of works, lest anyone should boast.*[78]

There is no work we can do which will impress God so much that it would cause Him to redeem us and bring us to heaven. All attempts to perform good works in order to earn our way into heaven are merely religious practices. As mentioned before, Jesus hates religion because it never brings anybody closer to God. Religion never involves a relationship with God. What we need to keep in mind is the lesson found in the very next verse:

> *For we are His workmanship,*
> *created in Christ Jesus for good works,*
> *which God prepared beforehand*
> *that we should walk in them.*[79]

One of the distinguishing characteristics of God is that *He declares the end from the beginning, and from ancient times things that are not yet done.*[80] That means God knows what is going to happen before it happens. God knows we will receive His free gift of salvation before we ever decide to accept it. So, He prepares good works ahead of time for us to do after we're born-again. This is God's means of allowing us to be workers together with Him.

If you ask a Christian if they are in a full-time ministry, the answer will most likely be "No," unless they are a missionary, pastor a church, or are on the staff of a particular ministry group. This, of course, is an incorrect answer. As born-again believers, we are all responsible for growing in our relationship with the Lord. As our relationship with God grows, we are to learn from Him what are the good works which He has already prepared for us to do. All Christians are supposed to be involved in full-time ministry.

Take notice that these are not works we come up with; these are works God has already prepared for us to do. God is waiting for us to grow in our relationship with Him so He can reveal these works to us at the proper time. Our responsibility is to *be diligent to present yourself approved to God, a worker who does not need to be ashamed, rightly dividing the word of truth.*[81]

Ambassadors of Christ

The good works which God prepares for each of us to walk in involve our responsibilities as *ambassadors of Christ*.[82] As ambassadors, we are to be focused on three major efforts: establishing His covenants[83], fulfilling the counsel of His will[84], and declaring His truth[85] in the world we live in today.

When Adam and Eve rebelled, the authority we once had in the world we live in was handed over to Satan, *the ruler of this* world.[86] In order for God to re-establish the authority of His Word in this world, He needs someone living in this world to be willing to rebel against Satan's authority. He needs someone who will establish the authority of His Word in any situation.

Yes, God owns this world. Satan only has a lease on the world, but that lease makes him the ruler of this world. God has the authority to intervene at any time He likes. But God prefers all those who are born-again to be workers together with Him, helping Him re-establish His *boqer* in a world filled with Satan's *erev*. As we pray according to the Word of God, we do become workers together with Him in that process.

As people who pray, we must be careful to be ambassadors who properly represent the Coming King. We must learn to be workers together *with* God. We must not be one who errantly takes God's Word and strikes out on his own, attempting to make a situation become what he *thinks* God would want it to be.

Sometimes we think we can do it all for the Lord. We must remember, *we are God's workmanship, created in Christ Jesus for good works, <u>which God prepared</u>*

beforehand, that we should walk in them.[87] God will lead us into the good works that He has already prepared for us to do. We can't rush out ahead of God and call for Him to catch up with us. It is a relationship, and we need to walk with Him as He leads us into those already-prepared-for-us good works.

Our authority to pray the Word of God into a situation lies in God, not in ourselves. When we pray the Word of God into a situation, we should do so under His leading. Only then have we become workers together with Him. Please notice whose Word and power are at work—not ours! God will cause His Word and His power to work according to His plans and purposes, which most likely will include other factors and situations of which we are totally unaware.

Praying by God's Word

We all go through situations in life. By now, we should know that God has something to say about those situations, something about how He can help us come through them in victory. We must learn to wait on the Lord, spending time in His presence and in His Word. Then we can bring the situation before Him and wait to hear what He has to say about it in His Word. Remember: *hearing comes by the Word of God.*[88] Learn to listen to the Holy Spirit. He will tell you what Scriptures will apply in your situation. God will tell you the process for removing the *erev* and restoring

His *boqer*. Then you can begin praying the Word of God into the situation.

Most prayers will fall into four general categories:

1. Salvation and spiritual growth.
2. Healing and deliverance.
3. Mammon: the influence material good and finances have on an individual, a family, and society.
4. Relationships: marriage, business, governmental, and others.

Conduct a topical Bible study of these four areas. Find out what the Word of God says about them. Then, as you pray about any of these situations, you will have a foundation of Scriptural understanding which the Holy Spirit can use to direct you in prayer. Be sure to let the Holy Spirit show you which Scriptures will apply in a particular situation. Don't pick and choose them yourself just because you think you already understand the situation. God knows far more details than you do. Let Him direct you in applying His Word.

In whichever of these categories your prayers fall, your will need to wait on the Holy Spirit and hear from Him. He will show you which Bible verses you should pray over that situation in order to expose and remove the *erev* and restore and increase God's *boqer*. This means that just as you took the time to learn the attributes of the Word of God, you will need to take time to hear what God has to say about each of these categories. This is the value of spending time daily in the Word. Please note carefully that the results of this kind of prayer are achieved:

1. Not based on any value in our own character or nature, but by us pleading the merits of God's Son, Jesus Christ.
2. Not by our own strength or power, but by the power of His Holy Spirit.
3. Not by our own goodness or righteousness, but by the righteousness that is from God by faith in the covenant Blood of Jesus Christ.
4. Not in our own words, or works, or wisdom, but by the Holy Spirit empowered *boqer* of God's Word restoring His order and unity in the situation.

The entire process involves taking time to lay the situation out before God and listen to the Holy Spirit in order to hear what Scriptures He would like applied in the situation. Then we are to patiently and consistently pray God's Word until the situation is restored to the order and unity God desires. You may be surprised at the means and methods God uses to repair and restore a situation. Pray in faith, *knowing* how faithful God is to His Word. Pray in faith, knowing that *God magnifies His Word above all His name*. Pray in faith, knowing God will not break His Word and His Word will fail:

So shall My word be that goes forth from My mouth;
it shall not return to Me void,
but it shall accomplish what I please, and it shall prosper
in the thing for which I sent it.[89]

Remember that learning to pray is a process, and all processes involve practice. Learning to pray is simply a means of building a stronger relationship with the Lord. As your relationship grows, your prayers increase in strength and yield more fruit for His Kingdom. Beyond bearing more fruit, our real goal and genuine joy are getting to know God more and more:

I do not cease ... making mention of you in my prayers:
that the God of our Lord Jesus Christ, the Father of glory,
may give to you the spirit of wisdom and revelation
in knowing Him.[90]

Sometimes when the Holy Spirit will have you step aside and stay out of the whole process. He will not show you what Word applies in the situation. You must stand aside and let the Holy Spirit choose the people He would like to pray in that situation. Your responsibility will be to continue to worship and build your relationship with the Lord. God may be taking you through a process of change and growth as well. Be patient, be thankful, and be willing to be instructed and redirected in prayer. The goal is to produce the fruit the Lord desires, not the fruit we think needs to be produced. Which brings us again to the process of...

Pruning

Let's build on what we learned about pruning from the lesson in chapter two:

*I am the true vine, and My Father is the vinedresser.
Every branch in Me that does not bear fruit
He takes away; and every branch that bears fruit
He <u>prunes</u>, that it may bear more fruit.
You are already <u>clean</u>
because of the word which I have spoken to you.*

Both words, "prunes" and "clean", are from the same Greek term, *kathario*, which simply means "to cleanse". God's Word is designed to show you what to remove from your life, and what to bring into your life. Part of the answer to your prayer may involve going through this pruning process. Yield. Allow God to work. The entire pruning process is designed to strengthen your relationship with the Lord and bring you to the place of bearing more fruit.

The pruning process requires that we *humble ourselves under the mighty hand of God*.[91] God instructs us to *buy the truth, and do not sell it, also wisdom and instruction and understanding.*[92]

Through the process of learning obedience and discipline, humbling yourself under the mighty hand of God, you are "buying Truth." What is truth, you may ask? Jesus provided the answer: *God's Word is Truth.*[93] You are settling once and for all, by the Holy Spirit's lessons, the validity and reliability of God's Word in your life. In the natural, we buy an investment and sell it later on for a profit (hopefully!) In our spiritual life, the purchase of the Truth of God's Word is an investment we must never, ever sell! Remember that the goal of God's pruning process is the production of fruit. In order to bear more fruit we must:

1. Grow our faith - our understanding that God says what He means and means what He says.
2. Build our relationship with the Lord.
3. Learn to apply His Word properly in order to remove the *erev* and increase His *boqer* in our lives.

God's Word Is Profitable

Let's look at one more attribute of the Word of God that will help us understand the value of His pruning process. It will also help us understand how the Lord accomplishes this process using His Word.

> *All Scripture is given by inspiration of God, and is profitable for doctrine, reproof, correction, instruction in righteousness, that the man of God may be complete, thoroughly equipped for every good work.*[94]

The first thing we should understand is that all Scripture comes from God. Literally, all Scripture is "God-breathed." Second, this verse tells us exactly what God's Word is profitable for:

- doctrine: which tells us what is right

- reproof: which tells us what is not right
- correction: which tells us how to get it right
- and instruction in righteousness: which tells us how to keep it right.[95]

In any situation we may face, we can trust God to show us in His Word the right actions to take and the right words to speak. God's Word will help us determine where we've gotten off track, and how to get back on track. By putting action to our faith in the Word of God, by applying His Word to our lives and living by it, we learn how to restore His order and produce His fruit. Third, this verse tells us the purpose of God's Word in His pruning process:

1. To make the man of God complete, perfect.
2. To make the man of God thoroughly equipped and thoroughly furnished for good works.

Biblical Examples of Praying by God's Word

Let's look at a couple examples of praying by God's Word found in the Bible. Our first example will be from Acts chapter four. Here we see the religious authorities of that day on a campaign to arrest and kill the disciples, attempting to prevent any preaching and teaching in the name of Jesus. Peter and John had just healed a lame man by the power found in Jesus' name. As a result, they were arrested and severely threatened before finally being released.

Upon their release, Peter and John went immediately to the rest of their group. They told them all that the religious leaders had said to them, all the threats and injunctions against preaching about anything using the name of Jesus. The disciples knew that these threats and injunctions were not meaningless. They knew that the religious leaders were not only capable of, but intent on carrying them out, even to the point of killing any disciple of Jesus. Their first response to the threats was praying the Word of God into the situation.

Lord, You are God, who made heaven and earth and the sea, and all that is in them, who by the mouth of Your servant David have said: Why do the nations rage, and the people plot vain things? The kings of the earth took their stand, and the rulers were gathered together against the LORD and against His Christ.

For truly against Your holy Servant Jesus, whom You anointed, both Herod and Pontius Pilate, with the Gentiles and the people of Israel, were gathered together to do whatever Your hand and Your purpose determined before to be done.

Now, Lord, look on their threats, and grant to Your servants that with all boldness they may speak Your Word, by stretching forth Your hand to heal, and that signs and wonders may be done through the name of Your holy Servant Jesus.[96]

They prayed using the Word of God found in Psalm 2, which applied to the situation they faced. God had just completed His plan of redemption for mankind. Jesus Christ, the Lamb of God, had died on the Cross and been raised from the dead, opening the way for all men to be born-again into the Kingdom of God. It was a plan God had prophetically revealed a little at a time since the day Adam and Eve rebelled in the Garden of Eden. God's work of redemption was finally complete, yet all the world and world leaders still fought against it. The disciples recognized this as they prayed the Word of God:

Why do the nations rage, and the people plot a vain thing?
The kings of the earth set themselves,
and the rulers take counsel together,
against the LORD and against His Anointed, saying,
Let us break their bonds in pieces
and cast away their cords from us.

Notice that they identified "the kings of the earth... and rulers" - Herod and Pontius Pilate - who *"counsel together against the Lord and against His Anointed"*. Do we recognize the rulers of the world today who still set themselves against the Lord and against His Christ? Be careful to recognize, not just the men, but the spiritual powers behind the men.

The disciples also identified those among the masses who agreed with these world rulers—*the Gentiles and the people of Israel.* Today, it doesn't appear that it will be long before the False Prophet, the False World-Leader, and those nations aligned with them will once again take counsel together against the Lord and against His Anointed.

Notice carefully the next part of the disciple's prayer. They acknowledge, not the work of those fighting against God's Anointed, but the fact that God knew about all of this in advance and even though people and nations were resisting Him, He would still see to it that everything works out according to His purpose. These kings of the earth and rulers would only be able to do *whatever Your hand and Your purpose determined before to be done*.

It has been mentioned previously that one of the unique identifying characteristics of God is that He *declares the end from the beginning, and from ancient times things that are not yet done, saying, 'My counsel shall stand, and I will do all My pleasure'.*[97] Under the direction of the Holy Spirit, this was another Scripture they were including in their prayer.

Finally, we should notice that they did not ask God to strike down or destroy the men who opposed them. The disciples had the understanding that God *is longsuffering toward men, not willing that any should perish but that all should come to repentance.*[98] They understood the love and power of God available to work in anyone. (In fact, if you look at some of the things Pilate said and did during the trial of Jesus, there is cause to believe we might see him in heaven.)

What the disciples asked God to do was this: as they applied God's Word to their situation in prayer, they asked the Lord to give them boldness to speak his Word, boldness to preach and teach in the name of Jesus by reinforcing their preaching and teaching with signs, wonders, and healings. In other words, they asked for the evidence and fruit of God's plan of redemption to be made manifest in their boldness to preach the death and resurrection of Jesus Christ!

God's answer was immediate. You will experience immediate answers to prayer from time to time, although not always as dramatic as this. The place they were in was shaken, they were filled with the Holy Spirit, and they spoke the Word of God with boldness. The *erev* - disorder, chaos, misinformation, and lies - of the threats and injunctions against preaching and teaching in the name of Jesus in that situation was removed. God's *boqer* - His order, unity, information, and truth was restored and made manifest. The multitude who believed were of one heart and soul, the apostles gave witness to the resurrection of the Lord Jesus with great power, and great grace was upon them all.[99]

Praying by the Word of God works! The disciples faced a situation which could prohibit them from preaching the truth about the death and resurrection of Jesus. They overcame that situation by praying the Word of God.

Example Two: Zechariah

After Israel's 70-year exile in Babylon, the people were allowed to return home to their land and to Jerusalem. Only about fifty thousand decided to make the trip back home. Upon their return, one of the first tasks they needed to accomplish was the rebuilding of the altar and the temple.

Actual construction of the temple was under the direction of Zerubbabel and Joshua. Zechariah and Haggai were God's prophet assigned to encourage and motivate the people to complete the building of the temple. The rebuilding of the altar proceeded apace with few problems. After they finished the altar, work began on the temple. It was at this time that Zechariah received God's Word about rebuilding the temple which culminated with a word of encouragement from the Lord:

> *Therefore thus says the LORD:*
> *I am returning to Jerusalem with mercy;*
> *My house shall be built in it,*
> *says the LORD of hosts.*[100]

The foundation for the temple was laid in 536 B.C. However, their neighbors, the Samaritans, were opposed to the idea of rebuilding the temple. (Notice: the Samaritans were opposed to the will of God.) The Samaritans were even able to obtain a restraining order from the Persian government prohibiting construction work. Faced with this opposition, the people who were building the temple became indifferent about completing the task, and lethargy set in.

Zechariah continued with prophetic words of motivation from the Lord, encouraging Zerubbabel and Joshua and the people to finish the work on the temple. There is one particular Word of the Lord we need to look at, and it is one we are probably already familiar with:

This is the word of the LORD to Zerubbabel:
Not by might nor by power, but by My Spirit,
says the LORD of hosts. Who are you, O great mountain?
Before Zerubbabel you shall become a plain!
And he shall bring forth the capstone with shouts of
"Grace, grace to it!"[101]

Notice that the enemy to God's plans and purposes had generated quite a bit of *erev*. It was enough to bring work on the temple to a standstill. And what was the Lord's response to the *erev* of the enemy? He spoke the Holy Spirit-empowered *boqer* of His Word to remove the *erev*. In a prophetic word of encouragement to Zerubbabel, who was to oversee the completion of the temple construction, God gave him the Word to speak over the entire process: *"Grace! Grace!"*

In this prophetic Word, God assured Zerubbabel that the temple would be completed, but not by the power of men, nor by military might against the Samaritans and

Persians. It would be completed by the Holy Spirit removing every obstacle of *erev* standing in opposition to the building of the temple. And that would be accomplished by Zerubbabel and the people working together with God, praying His grace into the situation!

What was the Word of God which Zechariah and Zerubbabel were to pray over the work for the rebuilding of the temple? "Grace! Grace!" That's all, just, "Grace! Grace!" But it was God's Word! It was the Holy Spirit-empowered *boqer* of God's Word that removed the *erev* and restored God's order, unity, information, and truth in the situation.

The foundation of the temple was laid 536 B.C. The temple was completed in 516 B.C. It took twenty years! Those men spoke "Grace!" over the entire process for twenty years. You will experience immediate answers to prayer from time to time as the disciples did in Acts 4. You will also experience periods of time that require your patience and determination in praying God's Word over the situation. What it amounts to is a test of your faith. Do you really believe God says what He means and means what He says? Do you really believe that God watches over His Word to perform it and that His Word will not return to Him void without accomplishing the purpose for which He sent it? Tests of faith are designed to draw us closer in our relationship with God and to make us more confident than ever that God says what He means and means what He says.

Know How to Pray the Word

> *My brethren, count it all joy*
> *when you fall into various trials,*
> *knowing that the testing of your faith produces patience.*[102]

Notice in the very next verse, the end products of a test of our faith,

> *But let patience have its perfect work,*
> *that you may be perfect and complete,*
> *lacking nothing.*[103]

One Last Consideration

> *Bless the LORD, you His angels, who excel in strength,*
> *who do His Word, heeding the voice of His Word.* [104]

God's angels are eagerly waiting for Him to speak His Word so they can perform it. There are angels standing by us. They are waiting for us to hear what the Holy Spirit is saying, and then to pray those words so they can perform them. Our responsibility is not to speak out Bible verses presumptuously, but to hear what the Holy Spirit is saying and pray accordingly. We must beware of presumptuous words! Remember what the Lord told Zerubbabel:

> *Not by might, nor by power*
> - not by man's strength or effort -
> *but by My Spirit, says the Lord of hosts.*

The Lord of armies of angels will accomplish His Word and His desire, with you or without you. Your part is to hear the Holy Spirit and obey. Real prayer requires a growing personal relationship with the Lord.

The foundation of prayer is knowing God!

Restoring Order in a Chaotic World

• APPENDIX A •

Hope: Faith Aimed at the Future

WE LIVE IN A FALLEN WORLD RULED BY EVIL. As Christians, we are to be a light shining in the darkness. We are to give people who dwell in darkness the light of hope. The best definition I've ever heard for hope is this: *Hope is faith aimed at the future.*

This book has endeavored to help you understand what real faith is. Real faith is knowing that what God says in the Bible has always been true, is true now, and will always be true in the future. And it is God's truth, under the direction of the Holy Spirit, that will restore order in a chaotic life and a chaotic world.

God's Word gives us hope, it shows us what can be; it shows us the kind of life God intended for us to live. Everyone has something in their life they wish was better, a relationship, health, finances, business. God's desire is for us to have His best life. We all "hope" for the best. But we do that in the sense of "wishing" for the best. Real hope is

Appendices

not the same as wishing. There is a substance, an underlying power, in real hope.

Consider This

Faith is believing that God's Word is true, and worthy of our complete trust. It is not just believing, but understanding that God says what He means, and means what He says. *Hope* is our faith in God's Word aimed at the future.

Genuine hope involves applying God's Word to a chaotic situation. It may be a chaotic relationship, a health issue, a financial issue, business problem, government, education, or "whatever" kind of problem. True hope applies God's Word to the chaos under the direction of the Holy Spirit, with the full expectation that the Word of God empowered by His Holy Spirit will produce the results God said it would. True hope is faith aimed at the future. This is the hope found in Hebrews 11:1,

> *Faith is the substance of things hoped for,*
> *the evidence of things not seen.*

Faith understands Isaiah 55:11 when God says,

> *So shall my Word be that goes forth from My mouth,*
> *it shall not return to Me void,*
> *but it shall accomplish what I please,*
> *and it shall prosper in the thing for which I sent it.*

Under the direction of the Holy Spirit, faith applies the

Hope: Faith Aimed at the Future

Word of God to a situation with the full expectation – the hope – of achieving God's purpose, plans, and results. Does this require diligence and patience? Yes. Two examples were given in this book. One where the results were instantaneous, and one where patience and persistence were required. You will experience both. James 1:2-8 provides more perspective,

Count it all joy when you fall into various trials,
knowing that the testing of your faith produces patience.
But let patience have its perfect work,
that you may be perfect and complete lacking nothing.
If any of you lacks wisdom, let him ask of God,
who gives to all liberally and without reproach,
and it will be given to him.

But let him ask in faith, with no doubting,
for he who doubts is like a wave of the sea
driven and tossed by the wind.
For let not that man suppose
that he will receive anything from the Lord;
he is a double-minded man, unstable in all his ways.

With these things in mind, there is one prayer which will produce instant results – every time. I guarantee you will not have to wait one second for God to answer this prayer.

There may be some who read this book who do not truly know the Lord Jesus. Part of the chaos and lies of this world include the thinking that God is not important, that

Appendices

even acknowledging Him, let alone knowing Him, carries no benefit. People go through nearly impossible mental contortions and gymnastics to avoid having any sense of responsibility toward God.

You may be a person of high rank in this world. Or of low rank. It makes no difference. Today, all of man's efforts are bent on finding a means of defeating death. Of gaining, not just a longer life, but an eternal life. The lie of the world says, "Through the advancements of science, you can be like God, and live forever."

Here's the problem with that lie: you are a three-part being: you are a spirit, you have a soul, and you live in a body. Your spirit and soul are already going to live forever. The only question is, where? In what "retirement village" will you spend eternity? Heaven or hell?

The only part of you that is going to die is your body. Today there are men and women of science, philosophy, higher learning, and so forth, who think they are going to take over the evolutionary process and lead mankind into the next step: immortality. They think they are going to create a new kind of man, a transhuman, or as pointed out in chapter one, "homo deus." Since evolution itself is a lie, they will never achieve this goal.

Even if scientist could achieve immortality, why would anyone want to live in a world where physical bodies can be reparied, but a person's soul and spirit are still dead?

Hope: Faith Aimed at the Future

Imagine living in a world where everyone is free to pursue an immoral lifestyle without having to face the consequences. A world where people can pursue whatever evil they desire with no cost.

Among those who truly do not know Christ, the spirit and soul they now possess is already dead, ruined and destroyed by sin and rebellion against God. It is our spirit and soul that we need to be concerned about giving life to, not our bodies. But we are incapable of achieving that goal on our own by *any* means.

Here's the good news. Jesus did not come to Earth to restore our spirit, nor to renovate it, or make it better. He came to give us a brand-new spirit. That new spirit will ultimately get a new body and we will live forever in heaven. Our old spirit, if left in its current condition, will never get another body, and we will spend all eternity in hell.

The amazing thing is, the choice is ours! Let's see, we can attempt to use science to re-work our own body - which would never be fully functional because we cannot improve upon the original design – and leave our spirit and soul in their current, unregenerate state of sin and wickedness, and end up spending eternity in hell. Or, we can choose to let the Author of Life Himself give us a new spirit and soul which are free from sin and wickedness, and then at the appropriate time, provide us with a new body which will last forever. Luke 9:24-25 puts it this way:

Appendices

> *For whoever desires to save his life will lose it,*
> *but whoever loses his life for My sake and the gospel's*
> *will save it.*
> *For what will it profit a man if he gains the whole world,*
> *and loses his soul…*
> *Or what will a man give in exchange for his soul…*
> *What profit is it to a man if he gains the whole world,*
> *and is himself destroyed or lost…*

It's not really a tough choice. Remember, God means what He says and says what He means. So, when He says, *"Whoever believes in the Lord Jesus will not be put to shame"*, and *"Whoever calls on the name of the Lord will be saved"*, He absolutely means it. For those who decide to choose God's upgrades over man's upgrades, Romans 10:9-10 tells you what you need to do to receive a new spirit and be born-again:

1. Believe in your heart that God raised Jesus from the dead.
2. Say out loud, "Jesus be my Lord."

And you will be saved. Yes, it is that easy. This is the prayer mentioned above, which is always answered on the spot! You can pray a prayer as simple as this:

Lord God, it was You who created me; it was You who pursued me relentlessly with all Your Love, and it was You who died on the Cross for me, paying the penalty for all my sins.

Lord, I yield my heart, my soul, and my mind to You

and Your Love. I believe with all my heart that God raised Jesus from the dead.

Jesus, I yield to Your Love, bowing my heart before You, and I ask You to be my Lord.

Thank You, Lord. I am a recipient of Your Love right here, right now.

Lord, your Word says that by Your power, when I receive Jesus as my Lord, I become Your child. Your Word says that in Christ Jesus I have become a new creation.

Thank You, Father, my old life is over and my new life in Christ Jesus has begun. Amen.

Here is what God says about what you've just prayed:

Most assuredly, I say to you,
he who hears My word
and believes in Him who sent Me
has everlasting life,
and shall not come into judgment,
but has passed from death to life.[105]

As many as received Him,
to them He gave the right to become children of God,
to those who believe in His name:
who were born,
not of blood, nor of the will of the flesh,
nor of the will of man, but of God.[106]

Awesome! Your new life starts *now*!

Appendices

On (today's date): _____,

(name): _____ was born-again as a child of the Living God.

Tips for growing in this new life and the new relationship you've just begun.

1. Remember, it's a relationship! Eternal life is knowing God, not knowing about God (John 17:3). Getting to know God takes time, just as it does with any other person.

2. Pursue your new relationship with the Lord by getting into His Word. By this, I mean two things:

    a. Study and meditate His Word. Get good resource materials, like the Blue Letter Bible app, and use them.

    b. Read portions of His Word each day, without study; just take time getting to know your Savior. It doesn't take enormous amounts of time. Just begin with five or ten minutes a day. It will grow from there.

3. Learn to pray. Prayer is just talking with God. This book was written to help you learn to pray. Communication is a two-way street, so make sure you also take the time to listen. Remember how

you learn to hear God: *Hearing comes by the Word of God* (Rom. 10:17). God will speak to you through His Word. As He does, learn to be obedient and apply His Word to your life. Begin using the Holy Spirit quickened life in God's Word to remove the *erev* – the disorder, chaos, lies, and misinformation, and to increase God's *boqer* – his order, unity, Truth, and information in your life - spirit, soul, and body.

4. Get around some other believers and begin to fellowship with them. Find and become part of a local church, one that sticks with the truth of God's Word and is actively advancing the Kingdom of God. You've just become a member of the Body of Christ, therefore begin to *grow up in all things into Him who is the head* – Christ Jesus – *from whom the whole body, joined and knit together by what every joint supplies, according to the effective working by which every part does its share, causes growth of the body for the edifying of itself in love* (Ephesians 4:15-16).

5. Declare the goodness of God. As you begin to more fully realize what God has done, and continues to do for you, tell people! They need an example to understand, and a voice from which to hear the Truth. (Romans 10:14-17)

Appendices

Finally, for those of you, who at this moment have decided not to take God up on His offer of a new spirit and a new life, our prayer for you is this:

Father, please send whoever and whatever is needed across their paths to help them:

1. *Change the way they think (to "repent" means to change the way you think so you can live a different lifestyle.)*

2. *Believe Your Gospel:*

   a. *That Christ died for our sins according to Scripture.*

   b. *That He was buried.*

   c. *That He rose again on the third day according to Scripture.*

3. *Be saved – pray the prayer above.*

4. *Come to the knowledge of the Truth about sin, righteousness, and judgment.*

   a. *About sin because they do not believe in the Lord, Jesus Christ.*

   b. *About righteousness, because the Lord Jesus has gone to be with the Father and we see Him no more.*

   c. *About judgment, because the ruler of this world is judged.*

Hope: Faith Aimed at the Future

Father, please help them understand their genuine need for a Savior – why they need a Savior, and Who their Savior is. We ask it in the name of Jesus. Amen.

Appendices

• APPENDIX B •

Attributes of God's Word

*Study to shew yourself approved unto God,
a workman that doesn't need to be ashamed,
rightly dividing the word of truth.*
~ 2 Timothy 2:15

Here are one hundred verses which provide lessons on the attributes and characteristics of God's Word, and therefore, of God Himself. Use these verses to kick-start your relationship with the Lord.

Please be aware that while some of these verses do not use the term "word", they still refer to the attributes of God's Word and how it can be applied to life. When the term "word" is used in a verse, it will be left up to you to determine if it refers to *dabar* or *imrah*, or to *logos* or *rhema*. As you meditate on these verses, the other thing you will notice is how the Holy Spirit connects different verses together to help you understand the lessons and to enlarge your heart. A few examples of this are provided.

This is designed as a personal study of the attributes of

Appendices

God's Word, the verses aren't written out for you. You must look these verses up and allow the Holy Spirit to talk to you and guide your lesson. Keep in mind there are many more verses on this lesson. Don't stop with these verses, find your own and keep your personal relationship with God fresh and growing!

Old Testament
1. Deuteronomy 8:3
2. Deuteronomy 32:46-47
3. Joshua 1:8
4. Joshua 21:45
5. 1 Samuel 3:6-7, 21 (Notice how God reveals Himself.)
6. 2 Samuel 22:31
7. 2 Kings 20:19
8. Psalm 12:6
9. Psalm 18:30
10. Psalm 19:9-11
11. Psalm 33:4
12. Psalm 33:6
13. Psalm 89:34
14. Psalm 105:8
15. Psalm 105:19
16. Psalm 107:20
17. Psalm 119:9, 11
18. Psalm 119:16
19. Psalm 119:28
20. Psalm 119:50
21. Psalm 119:89
22. Psalm 119:105
23. Psalm 119:107
24. Psalm 119:116

Attributes of God's Word

25. Psalm 119:140
26. Psalm 119:160, 169
27. Psalm 119:162 (See Matthew 6:21; Luke 12:34!)
28. Psalm 138:2
29. Psalm 147:15
30. Proverbs 2:1ff
31. Proverbs 3:1-5
32. Proverbs 4:5
33. Proverbs 4:20-21ff
34. Proverbs 6:23
35. Proverbs 12:25
36. Proverbs 13:13
37. Proverbs 15:23
38. Proverbs 16:20
39. Proverbs 23:12
40. Proverbs 30:5
41. Ecclesiastes 8:4
42. Isaiah 40:8
43. Isaiah 46:9-10
44. Isaiah 50:4
45. Isaiah 55:10-11
46. Isaiah 59:21
47. Jeremiah 15:16
48. Jeremiah 23:29
49. Ezekiel 12:28
50. Micah 2:7

New Testament

51. Matthew 4:4
52. Matthew 12:37 (cf: Mark 8:38)
53. Mark 7:13
54. Mark 13:31 (c.f. Matthew 24:35; Luke 21:33)
55. Mark 16:20
56. Luke 4:32, 36

Appendices

57. Luke 7:7
58. Luke 8:11-15
59. Luke 11:28 (c.f. James 1:6)
60. John 1:1-5
61. John 6:63
62. John 6:68
63. John 8:51
64. John 14:23-24
65. John 15:1-8
66. John 17:17
67. Acts 12:24
68. Acts 14:3
69. Acts 19:20
70. Romans 10:17
71. Romans 15:18-19
72. 1 Corinthians 2:4-5
73. 1 Corinthians 2:13
74. 1 Corinthians 4:20
75. 2 Corinthians 1:20
76. 2 Corinthians 5:19
77. Ephesians 4:29
78. Ephesians 5:26 (c.f. John 17:17)
79. Ephesians 6:17
80. Philippians 2:16
81. Colossians 3:16-17
82. 1 Thessalonians 1:5
83. 1 Thessalonians 2:13
84. 2 Thessalonians 2:16-17
85. 2 Thessalonians 3:1
86. 1 Timothy 4:5-6
87. 2 Timothy 1:13
88. 2 Timothy 2:15
89. Titus 1:9
90. Hebrews 1:3
91. Hebrews 4:12, 14b
92. Hebrews 11:3

Attributes of God's Word

93. James 1:21-25 (Look into the Word so much, you remember who you are in Christ even when you're not looking into the Word.)
94. 1 Peter 1:23-25
95. 1 Peter 2:2-3
96. 2 Peter 1:19-21
97. 1 John 1:1-4
98. 1 John 2:3-5
99. Revelation 12:11
100. Revelation 19:13

Appendices

• APPENDIX C •

ENDNOTES

A Note From The Author

1. 1 Corinthians 2:3; Colossians 2:4
2. John 17:3
3. Matthew 7:23
4. John 7:38; Ephesians 2:10
5. Matthew 25:23

Chapter 1

6. Ecclesiastes 1:3-4
7. Ecclesiastes 1:9
8. Ecclesiastes 1:14
9. Ecclesiastes 2:11
10. Ecclesiastes 12:12-14
11. Colossians 2:8-9
12. Revelation 12:11
13. Matthew 6:24 (Jesus is not saying that we have to choose between God and mammon, one or the other; and if you choose God, you've chosen to be poor. What He is saying is that you must choose which one you will serve and which one will serve you. If you serve God, then you need to learn to rule and reign over mammon.)
14. Ecclesiastes 2:11
15. Ecclesiastes 1:9

Appendices

16. Genesis 3:5
17. Craig, William Lane, Humanism For Children. OnFaith. Retrieved May 29, 2017, from <https://www.onfaith.co/onfaith/2012/12/10/humanism-for-children/11669>
18. Ecclesiastes 1:3-4
19. Romans 6:19
20. 2 Corinthians 4:4
21. 2 Thessalonians 2:7
22. Ecclesiastes 12:12b
23. Ecclesiastes 12:13-14
24. John 17:15
25. Colossians 2:20
26. 2 Corinthians 6:1
27. 2 Corinthians 5:20
28. 2 Chronicles 7:14
29. Exodus 20:7
30. 2 Corinthians 3:18
31. Romans 12:2
32. Matthew 5:16
33. Philippians 3:13-14

Chapter 2

34. Revelation 12:11
35. Hebrews 1:3
36. Hebrews 11:3
37. Psalm 33:6
38. Genesis 1:26
39. Ephesians 4:24
40. Romans 8:29
41. 2 Corinthians 3:18
42. James 3:3-5
43. Proverbs 13:3
44. Matthew 12:37
45. Proverbs 18:21

Endnotes

46. <https:ww.google.com/search?q=what+is+faith&ie=utf-8&oe=utf-8>
47. Ephesians 2:8
48. Romans 3:23
49. Romans 6:21, 23
50. Luke 17: 5
51. Luke 17:6
52. Romans 10:17
53. John 17:3
54. Romans 8:29
55. 2 Corinthians 3:18
56. Colossians 3:9-10
57. Galatians 4:19
58. Proverbs 22:21
59. Luke 8:11
60. Colossians 1:23

Chapter 3

61. Psalm 145:1-3
62. Acts 3:16
63. Philippians 2:10
64. Ephesians 1:21
65. Machiavelli, Niccolò, *The Prince*, 1513.
66. Ibid.
67. Ibid.
68. Proverbs 12:22
69. Psalm 101:7
70. Jeremiah 1:12, KJV
71. Numbers 23:19
72. 1 Peter 1:15-16
73. Matthew 12:36
74. Luke 4:4
75. Matthew 5:14-16
76. Psalm 119:130

Appendices

Chapter 4
77. 2 Corinthians 6:1
78. Ephesians 2:8-9
79. Ephesians 2:10
80. Isaiah 46:10
81. 2 Timothy 2:15
82. 2 Corinthians 5:20
83. Deuteronomy 8:18
84. Ephesians 1:11; Romans 12:1-2; Colossians 1:9
85. Psalm 40:10; 71:18; Acts 20:20, 27
86. John 14:30
87. Ephesians 2:10
88. Romans 10:17
89. Isaiah 55:11
90. Ephesians 1:16-17
91. 1 Peter 5:6
92. Proverbs 23:23
93. John 17:17
94. 2 Timothy 3:16-17
95. Wiersbe, Warren W, *Be Ready, Living In The Light Of Christ's Return*, pg. 71, Aug. 2010.
96. Acts 4:24-30
97. Isaiah 46:10
98. 2 Peter 3:9
99. Act 4:33
100. Zechariah 1:16
101. Zechariah 4:6-7
102. James 1:2-3
103. James 1:4
104. Psalm 103:20

Hope: Faith Aimed At The Future
105. John 5:24
106. John 1:12-13

www.ingramcontent.com/pod-product-compliance
Lightning Source LLC
LaVergne TN
LVHW041632070426
835507LV00008B/583